VOICE-OVER

VOICE-OVER
Norman MacCaig

Chatto & Windus LONDON

Published in 1988 by Chatto & Windus Ltd
30 Bedford Square, London WCIB 3RP

British Library Cataloguing in Publication Data
MacCaig, Norman
    Voice-over.
    I. Title
    821'.914   PR6063.A

    ISBN 0 7011 3313 9

Photoset in Linotron Sabon by
Rowland Phototypesetting Ltd
Bury St Edmunds, Suffolk

Printed in Great Britain by
Redwood Burn Ltd
Trowbridge, Wiltshire

Contents

Between mountain and sea

Honey and salt – land smell and sea smell,
as in the long ago, as in forever.

The days pick me up and carry me off,
half-child, half-prisoner,

on their journey that I'll share
for a while.

They wound and they bless me
with strange gifts:

the salt of absence,
the honey of memory.

Low tide

Under six inches of water
pebbles, each one of them noble
in the heraldic colours of their ancestry.

Time sits weaving
and unweaving an endless tapestry
for a Ulysses who will one day come.

As I will – not this caricature
who wades in six inches of water.
My true self, my aimless wanderer.

I pick up a pebble and watch
its colours fade – and put it back. Full tide
won't dull its invisible shining.

Repulsive death washes into my mind.
It won't dull the invisible shinings there –
dead friends, noble in the last certainty.

Small boy

He picked up a pebble
and threw it into the sea.

And another, and another.
He couldn't stop.

He wasn't trying to fill the sea.
He wasn't trying to empty the beach.

He was just throwing away,
nothing else but.

Like a kitten playing
he was practising for the future

when there'll be so many things
he'll want to throw away

if only his fingers will unclench
and let them go.

Slow evening

Night is long in coming. Its soft feet
pause at the horizon. Stars wait
for the light to go out, to perform
their brilliant rituals on their dark stage.

My mind that was sleepy with waiting
begins to waken, to feel small movements
like the tiny waves fudged in a glass of water
carried by a child.

Light drains away. – But there,
sudden windows appear on dark buildings,
small universes wheeling nonchalantly
with Saturn and the tilted Plough.

Sealubber

Far on any ocean, with horizons
always the same distance away,
there's an Odysseus, a big bold fellow
made of bronze or a scruffy gray one
with a chewed moustache.
They know where they're going
even if there's no harbour there to creep into.

Do I envy them their hard way
with dissatisfactions and boredoms, their exchange
of the paradox of friends and of lovers
for the loneliness they're in love with?

I nid-nod in my rocking harbour.
It has a welter of waves in it
that no-one can see, that has
terror enough. And I sail
on the never-ending voyage
to where I am already, dizzy
with beautiful Troys and
dangerous Circes and dark journeys
to the land of the shades.

Divider

Greek Atlas is all of us.
He feels the earth
being pushed into him
by the heavenly sky.

But stubbornly
he keeps them apart.
He stands, his own limbo,
always stubborn, always complaining.

Sleepy time

The lamp hisses: a lullaby hiss.
The fire cradles two little flames.
And the world's one room; time
has escaped from the ticking clock.

Somebody sighs. A hand dangles
from a chair arm;
and a man's head droops.
The night outside creeps into it.

Perfect evening, Loch Roe

I pull the boat along gently. In the stern
Donald tucks his long rod under his arm
and lights his pipe.

Behind my right shoulder
the cliff Salpioder holds out
its anvil nose
over the sea.

The distances of other times,
the unmeasurable ones,
have withdrawn into nowhere at all.

– A sudden clamour. Oystercatchers
fly off from a gray rock –
their orange-red beaks; their wingbars flashing white.

The desires of other times too
have disappeared
behind the desires that lay beyond them.

And the dreams of other times
are huddled in their false country,
exiles returned to their homeland.

I feel something like love.
I can spare it, for the source of it all
is waiting, there, in the squat cottage.

Compare and contrast

The great thinker died
after forty years of poking about
with his little torch
in the dark forest of ideas,
in the bright glare of perception,
leaving a legacy of fourteen books
to the world
where a hen disappeared
into six acres of tall oats
and sauntered unerringly
to the nest with five eggs in it.

Chauvinist

In all the space of space
I have a little plot of ground
with part of an ocean in it
and many mountains.

It's there I meet my friends
and multitudes of strangers.
Even my forebears dreamily visit me
and dreamily speak to me.

Of the rest of space
I can say nothing
nor of the rest of time, the future
that dies the moment it happens.

The little plot – do I belong to it
or it to me? No matter.
We share each other as I walk
amongst its flags and tombstones.

Mountain streamlet

Thin splash of water. There should be
red eyes in it or a shiver
of gold grains.

How tiny its water-nymphs would be.
It couldn't trundle away
even the head of Orpheus.
And Ophelia would step over it
singing her sad songs.

I look for the red eyes –
they're there, pebbles
among the white ones.

And gold grains? They're in my mind,
enriching me.

If only I could wrap up
its little music
and take it with me
to my city room.

I'd listen to it and,
if I were Wordsworth,
I'd write something called
Innocence and Independence.

On a croft by the Kirkaig

The cock, king of the croft, crowed,
tearing a jagged rip in the silence
that even the river washing by
had failed to disturb.

My mind was like the silence:
an equivalence of peace.

But the cock crowed, ushering in
another day at midday.
What day?

And into my mind came the man
with whom, so often, I'd sat by that river,
now in the most rounded silence of all
where no river shuffles by
and no cock will ever crow again.

I'm sad
but not sad only,
for I share his possessions
and therefore himself.

Cherishingly, I count three of them –
the equivalence of peace,
the cock, carved on tiptoe
on the gold coin of himself,
and the river bundling its sweet vocabulary
towards the swarming languages
of the sea.

Thinking of contradictions

Take away the contradictions
and what's left? Heaven.

Only the gods
could settle as happy natives
in that place of no contradictions,
that place of certainty, the place of peace.

And who'd want to be there anyway,
unable to enjoy the darling gifts
of rage, jealousy, cruelty, lust
and that power, the truly godlike one,
of destroying our own creations?

Old Highland woman

She sits all day by the fire.
How long is it since she opened the door
and stepped outside, confusing
the scuffling hens and the collie
dreaming of sheep?
Her walking days are over.

She has come here through centuries
of Gaelic labour and loves
and rainy funerals. Her people
are assembled in her bones.
She's their summation. *Before her time*
has almost no meaning.

When neighbours call
she laughs a wicked cackle
with love in it, as she listens
to the sly bristle of gossip,
relishing the life in it,
relishing the malice, with her hands
lying in her lap like holy psalms
that once had a meaning for her, that once
were noble with tunes
she used to sing long ago.

Memory

Over the turbulence of the world
flies the bird that stands for memory.
No bird flies faster than this one,
dearer to me
than the dove was to Noah – though it brings back
sometimes an olive branch, sometimes
a thorny twig without blossoms.

On the north side of Suilven

The three-inch-wide streamlet
trickles over its own fingers
down the sandstone slabs
of my favourite mountain.

Like the Amazon it'll reach the sea.
Like the Volga
it'll forget its own language.

Its water goes down my throat
with a glassy coldness,
like something suddenly remembered.

I drink
its freezing vocabulary
and half understand the purity
of all beginnings.

Foreboding in Eden

Is it my fault, delicate Eve,
that I'm a man called
Adam?

I'm in life and in love.
The painless wound in my side
has healed.
And I've finished naming the animals,
all but one.

But something's wrong. The night
groans and whirls
in the first storm of all.

Tomorrow will come. Wounded,
it'll thrash in the air.

– Till a silence falls and in it
we'll meet the maker of storms,
the maker of stillness.

Curlew

Yesterday, I saw a cousin of yours,
a whimbrel,
that, when close to, looks like yourself
seen at a distance.

But who could mistake its tittery call
for yours, brown bird, as you fly
trailing bubbles of music
over the squelchy hillside?

As desolate, as beautiful
as your loved places,
mountainy marshes and glistening mud-flats
by the stealthy sea.

Neighbour

His car sits outside the house.
It never goes anywhere. Is it
a pet?

When he goes for his morning paper
he makes a perfect right-angle
at the corner.

What does he do at home? Sit at attention?
Or does he stay in the lobby
like a hatstand?

Does his wife know she married
a diagram? That she goes to bed
with a faded blueprint?

When I meet him
he greets me with a smile
he must have bought somewhere.

His eyes are two teaspoons
that have been emptied
for the last time.

Highland barbecue

Darkness has come
snuffing the candles of distance,
binding the legs of the tall ash trees,
with black bandages.

By the Red Rock Pool
the youngsters of the village
have their barbecue going and near it
a bonfire of logs
and broken fishboxes. The flames jig
to the jigging of Jimac's accordion.

From a distance it looks like
a tiny, mediaeval hell – all that red,
those figures in the flicker.

But come close. It's a heavenly glebe
of charred sausages and laughter,
of young seraphs licking their fingers
and adding to the jewel heap
of praise-the-Lord
Coca-Cola tins.

They pay no heed, in their short-lived holiness,
to the gull over the bay
– rejected spirit
lamenting in the desolation
of the outer darkness.

Buzzard circling

The landscape wheels round
its centre – the buzzard that sees
a hill slide sideways,
a field spin round.

The buzzard wheels
round another, invisible centre,
the black hole that waits
for buzzard and hill –

that will suck in
all circumferences
to the place that was
before chaos was created.

New flood

For five days and nights
the windows have worn veils
of thin water.

We know the river
is making samurai sounds.
It's swollen, it's apoplectic.

But all we can hear
is the rain, sounding
like dwarfs rushing through thickets.

I'd feel like Noah, but for you,
woman of gentleness
stroking the pale dove.

A happiness

Each second is birds singing in every tree.
Not real birds. Not real trees.

And my room is mornings stretching on forever.
Not real mornings nor that real forever.

A plough went into the ground. Corn rose from it.
I saw that plough. I saw that corn.

They were real. But for this fragile moment
the plough turns over the soil into the future.

where the corn sways
that was cut down long ago.

Like you, like everyone

Forgive me, unknown creators,
forebears whose blood
flickers and dwindles in me.

Like you, I'm a leaf
that hangs down helpless
on the tree of my people.

And like you I move
in whatever wind blows
from whatever spaces.

Forgive the love I feel in only my way
and the griefs I suffer
in only my way of suffering.

For Time's microbes work ceaselessly,
changing you and me and everything
with no thought of forgivingness.

On Lachie's croft

On Lachie's croft the cock stands
under the wheelbarrow. What's wrong? – He's bedraggled.
Where are his military elegance,
his gauleiter manners, his insufferable conceit?
I'll call him rooster, it seems more fitting.

I, too, feel bedraggled and haphazard; something
has filched my compass, I'm breathing black air.
I look at that rooster, I look at me.

His hens scratch the ground, step back
and peer at the scratches. They make
motherly sounds, so cosy, so fireside.

But he opens his gummy eyes, looks at me
and utters, no tortured trumpet call,
but a barren croak.

I breathe black air, I poke at
my rumpled feathers, I can't stand on tiptoe.
How I miss my cosy brown hens.
How I miss their motherly clucking.
I'm master of nothing I survey.

Dark centre

The dust silvers and a wind from the corner
brings a dream of clarinets
into the thick orchestra. There's a place
sending messages across the river of people;
and the sullen wharves of buildings
begin to smell of bales and distances.

I have a sad place that nobody enters
but a ragged man hooking the air
with skinny fingers. I sit beside him sometimes,
feeling his despair. His loneliness
infects me.

But today's a day of clarinets and silver
under the lucky horseshoe of the sky.
I leave him and go into the whirlpools of light,
through a jazz of gardens and heliograph windows.

— That house is my monkish cell, my fortress.

I put the key in the door and stop,
terrified that the ragged man
is sitting in my chair with his skinny fingers
tangled in his lap.

On the pier at Kinlochbervie

The stars go out one by one
as though a bluetit the size of the world
were pecking them like peanuts out of the sky's string bag,

A ludicrous image, I know.

Take away the gray light.
I want the bronze shields of summer
or winter's scalding sleet.

My mind is struggling with itself.

That fishing boat is a secret
approaching me. It's a secret
coming out of another one.
I want to know the first one of all.

Everything's in the distance,
as I am. I wish I could flip that distance
like a cigarette into the water.

I want an extreme of nearness.
I want boundaries on my mind.
I want to feel the world like a straitjacket.

Apparition

Before me, the solid cone
of Ben Stack
looks in all directions at once
without needing to turn.

I climb and climb and climb,
disliked by a peregrine,
no friend to a lizard,
shunned by a hind
with two followers.

At the cairn I turn round and scan
the jumbled wilderness
of mountains and bogs and lochs,
South, East, North and then – West
– the sea

where a myth in full rig,
a great sailing ship, escaped
from the biggest bottle in the world,
glides grandly through the rustling water.

The tribes of men

They think they walk in their country.
They walk to it.

Ignorant of the earthquake already
swelling its muscles under their feet
or the spark that will bring down a whole forest.

They read the stars overhead
like patterns of stories. All childish tales.
Let them read the darkness between them.

Their country is the one they're walking to,
the one that's the darkness
where they'll hear not even the grass overhead.

They give birth and they murder. They make
music of tears and instruments.
Hate, love and boredom are their companions.

Let them relish them all. Let them be:
those exiled translators of reality
whom the grass neither forgets nor remembers.

Country cameo

Talking (like crows) of crows
three old men by a wall
in interesting attitudes.

The minister passes. He greets them.
They greet him
like doves.

When he's gone, they fall into
new interesting attitudes
and talk (like crows) of the minister.

Wild snowstorm

Men dressed like Laplanders
are digging and digging to free
the trapped dragon of the snowplough.

Are they digging in the inside
of a faulty TV screen? They make no sound
that can be heard.

Toss the snow up. Each shovelful
flocks and flies, scattering
to the next parish or settles

behind a wall, behind a boulder,
behind any steepness . . .
The dragon clears its throat

and roars and moves,
like a nightmare, forward
into a furious whiteness,

into a raging Christmas
where the angels scream and bellow
over all the Bethlehems in the world.

Other self, same self

Such warmth in my mind
where you talk and laugh
and drink drams
and walk amongst mountains

– though I touched your cold brow
on that wintry morning
that went away
and took you with it.

Sounds and silences

The gabbling river
talking to itself –
such garrulities.

– Even the quietest of nights
are never silent: hear
their shadows of sounds.

I've thought no silence
could be deeper than the one
in your sleeping self.

But heft that stone. It has
a language beyond our hearing,
a re-forming of crystals.

And you'll wake in the morning
the one I've known
and the new one, the always new one.

Man, rabbit and owl

To see you, little owl,
swallowing that baby rabbit
for two minutes of violent gulping . . .

I turn away,
I who have fed
on the bread of peace, tender slices
of happiness, comfits of sweet joy.

I look away into the rabbits' world.
They snuffle the air, rubbing together
the halves of their noses;
they rockinghorse forward
and sit straight up, following their ears.

You pay no heed, little owl,
but gulp down your comfits of pleasure,
your fur-ball of happiness,
your sum of present delights.

Too many lessons from one
non-philosopher to another . . .

I bless you from my other world
and walk away, whistling,
through a scatter of rabbits
bobbing their white scuts
into their dens of peace.

Over and over again

Tomorrow we'll meet again
as for the first time, though we've not crossed
the river that's both cruel and kind –
that Lethe the ancients spoke about.
And of the buried suns one will arrive
and make bright the fields
where Persephone must have passed:
so many the flowers.
We'll not shrink when we skirt
the entrance to the Underworld
nor be blinded by that shell sauntering in
on to the shore of everywhere.

All myths, with the truth of myths.
We'll do it our way –
with a look, with a touch
and with the space between words
where the truths live
that we can find no words for.

April Day in November, Edinburgh

The sun punches through the cloud gaps
with strong fists and the wind
buffets the buildings
with boisterous good will.

Bad memories are blown away
over the capering sea. Life
pulls up without straining
the jungle tangle between us
and the future.

Easy to forget
the last leaves thicken the ground
and the last roses are dying
in their sad, cramped hospitals.

For gaiety's funfair whirls
in the gray squares. Energy
sends volts from suburb to suburb.

And April, gay trespasser,
dances the dark streets of November,
Pied Piper leading a procession
of the coloured dreams of summer.

Plea not to be deserted

Have I taken all I can from you,
books of the masters, printed on the yellowing years?
I know you've hung songs on constellations
I can't visit and under my feet
your minerals are glowing that I can't reach,
dig as I might, furiously, in my midnight room.

Sneak cleverly from behind me, from between
my roving glances, as you did when Catullus
came smiling in and Dante, wrapped in a cloak
of light years, scattered so many shadows
with his white lucidities

I'm a man waiting to be ambushed.
Take time off to notice me, to step
from a doorway and slip into my hand
a tract of timelessness, a never-ending
exclamation, a single word, like the first one,
of continuous creation, of difficult universes.

Inside and out

In my head there's a book being written
about loneliness, who stares in a mirror
in her homeless home, watching
her limp hands, her frantic eyes.

Walking through buds and blossoms,
poor Spring, my Spring, is weeping. She sits by the pond
not heeding the swan sculptures. She leans
her head on the night's shoulder and weeps.

Take her to the window, someone. Make her see how
true Spring – gay in her finery, in a world smirking
in the latest fashion – goes smiling down the road
where even Time, at that corner, stands dressed to kill.

Is happiness to be found only in a world
of no mirrors? – where eyes look out only and relish
the cloud tumbling over the ears
of the milkman's horse sticking up through its battered
    hat?

Backward look

Call up for my contemplation
the black longships with their snakish heads
sliding into a Shetland bay:
– and their murderous, witty crews
whose speech was as laconic
as their swords and battleaxes.

Or Troy and highminded Hector
scaring his baby with his nodding, noble plume
– and the wooden horse, stolid outside the walls,
pregnant with flames and screaming women.

Or ugly Socrates, monolith-still
in the middle of the battle, brooding
on his beautiful, improbable abstractions:
see his hand, without a tremor,
raise the glass of hemlock to his truthful lips.

Or Luther, hammering those famous nails
into the Cathedral door
– and into the minds of men, driving them to scurry
with the Lord's book in their hands
to torture chambers and battlefields.

Or Captain Cook or Livingstone or Columbus
bringing to unknown countries
the goodies of civilisation,
every one sweet, every one poisonous.

History frightens me. It reminds me
of me and you
and everyone else.

If only I come to be, in its long story,

a word with brackets round it,
a word drowned in a footnote,
a word
whose meaning has been forgotten.

February — not everywhere

Such days, when trees run downwind,
their arms stretched before them.

Such days, when the sun's in a drawer
and the drawer locked.

When the meadow is dead, is a carpet,
thin and shabby, with no pattern.

and at bus stops people retract into collars
their faces like fists.

— And when, in a firelit room, mother looks
at her four seasons, at her little boy,

in the centre of everything, with still pools
of shadows and a fire throwing flowers.

A man and his dreams

I only wanted my dreams to stay
in the iron circle
of reason, of possibility.

They kept going off into far places.
They smouldered beyond horizons.

— But tomorrow will come
with hope, its little child.
And I'll walk in my friendly streets
past the small front gardens,
looking at the sooty snowdrops
and the fool's gold
of daffodils.

And the iron circle will tighten
till I'm content
with the smirched snowdrops
and the daffodils that never think
of Wordsworth's wild ones
and dance the best they can.

Crofter

Last thing at night
he steps outside to breathe
the smell of winter.

The stars, so shy in summer,
glare down
from a huge emptiness.

In a huge silence he listens
for small sounds. His eyes
are filled with friendliness.

What's history to him?
He's an emblem of it
in its pure state.

And proves it. He goes inside.
The door closes and the light
dies in the window.

Still is the night

I'm sleepless. I lie trying to hear
the house breathing, wondering
why the curtain trembles, wondering
what cracked a knuckle outside the door.

Still is the night? Not ever. Its creatures
scuttle and pounce and die.
A tree whispers to the window
and footsteps go by; there's a man on them.

Impossible to think of canoes paddling
on tropical lagoons or caravans
winding over mountain passes.
The night is nearness, it presses down on me.

A godlike car passes in a golden shower:
it throws a handful in through the window.
– Too much is going on. I think uneasily
of a hand twitching the bedclothes.

A room and a woman in it

It smells of old age,
of a past long dead.
Nothing has changed for so long.

How imagine that chair
is another place? The table
is rooted in years long past.

And the old woman, lonely and sad,
sits wrapped in a shawl of memories,
waiting for the latch to lift
and the door to open
to let in Time with his tall black hat
and a band of crape round his arm.

Crew

Three men are pulling
at the starboard oar,
the man I am and was
and the man I'll be.

The boat sails
to a blind horizon.
Who's pulling on the portside oar
that keeps our course straight?

Pull as we may
we're kept from turning
to port or starboard by that
invisible oarsman.

Little girl

She wept in a green corner.
The little girl ran into the garden
and sat shaking and weeping
between two bushes.

Because her mother wouldn't give her
a rabbit in a little hutch
with straw to lie on and a dinner
of lettuce and dandelions.

How could she know she would bear
the death of her mother,
the obscenities of wars,
the last illness, the first death?

— with what courage is
and the loss of innocence
and with no green corner
and few tears left for weeping?

Heavenly party

He watches the goddesses dancing
so gracefully and the gods
so elegantly – even, he thinks bitterly,
that lame-footed fellow over there.

He can't be bothered.
He's past it.

And he thinks of the good old days.
Turn into a swan? –
no bother.
A shower of gold? –
all in the night's work.

*I'm infected
with humanity*, he thinks,
knocking over his nectar.

Ganymede! he bellows.
The same again! A large one!

Poor Zeus.

It's always, always
the same again
in boring Olympus.

Two nights

The real night, the one
that keeps coming back on time,
never begins
with a gash of black.

As though, politely,
it makes a noise on the gravel
and coughs and knocks at the door
before coming in.

Not like the other one, that
on the most summer of days
gashes the light and pours through
a black dark with no moon, no stars.

Her illness

For this once I force myself
to write down the word *light*.
So many times in the last cloudy months
I've tried to and my mouth
said *dark*.

For the waters of Babylon
sound in my friendly river, my harp
hangs in a familiar tree.

I used not to care
that there never were unicorns
and that a phoenix was only
a metaphor on fire.
I knew that, but I loved them.

But truth has been stripped of its flesh,
its eyes, its gentle hands.
It reaches out an arm and lays
five cold bones on my knee.
It never stops smiling
with a changed smile.

End of her illness

The stones click their teeth in the darkness,
the darkness of memory, where a skeleton
burns its phosphorus and jeers
at the rising sun.

And animals stumble there, birds fall
with a cry on to the sour clods,
and even friends shrink to Tom Thumb puppets
jerkily greeting friends, jerkily shaking hands.

But now that memory has been rinsed
and laundered. The sun bleaches on curved bushes
and the whole air is a music I can hardly hear
but hear all the time.

A gentle miracle asked for shelter
and I received her in a house suddenly bright
whose shadows only made the brightness clearer.
What's night and day to me?

The unscalable cliff has vanished
as in a pantomime transformation and I
hold Cinderella by the hand and listen
to our friends applauding out there in the world.

Emblems

They went away, the sad times.
It wasn't I who turned them out of doors,
but another.

The swifts have returned. They've dropped
their burden of long journeys. With what joy
they scream over the rooftops.

Pour the coffee. Sit by the fire
that says *home*. Tomorrow we'll welcome
all the tomorrows there are to be.

Do you hear the swifts? They tie together
the bright light. They nest
in secret places.

Daybreak

Count the lights down,
those lustrous, trembling stars.

If therc's an hour whose father
was Proteus, this is it.

The night sky is turning into
a space of pearl. In the East

it faintly flushes, where the hidden sun
sends forward its gentle announcement.

And history, that hasn't slept, yawns
in his workshop – he'll make

a million things today
and be surprised by none of them.

There's one already – a milk bottle waiting
for the door of a house to open.

And another – a baby crying
in the first of all its minutes.

Seasonal notes – June

Kamikaze swifts dive-bomb the rooftops
(missing them every time) then soar
screaming and wheeling –
if they towed pencils behind them
they'd draw huge baskets in the sky.

Salmon waver behind boulders
and attack waterfalls
with elegant ferocity.

On mountains stags pose
beside lochs, still expecting
Landseer, then huffily
start grazing
beside a chuckling burn.

In the evening villages
men are sucked into pubs
to talk like ruminants
and drink like stirrup-pumps.

And the corn grows
gluttonously towards fruition,
towards the day when the combine harvester
clanks from a nightmare mind
and lurches into the field.

And all the uprising forces
will dwindle and die down,
leaving it to the sleeping earth
to dream them up again.

Getting where?

What so pure
as arrivals,
each a promise
of new beginnings?

We step into a place
we've never seen
or a place
where once we suffered.

And silly hope greets us, She says
What a beautiful Spring day
and smiles charmingly
among the falling leaves.

The dear green place

I quarter my little field.
It stretches from the fall of Troy
to this minute, but it's not cramped
in my skull.

Its natives, all artists, make shapes
out of words and sounds and colours
and anything solid. They have a basilisk eye
for clocks and calendars.

Not an eagle, me, but
an ancient sparrowhawk
dowdily perched on fenceposts
in any century.

Still, I pop up over the hedges
in a dashing way, looking to surprise
a mousy philosopher
or a scuttling poet.

The pleasing thing is
when I've devoured a warbling musician
and fly off, I hear him behind me
still practising Op.4 No.6.

This country makes a fool of ecology
and an ass of conservation.
It's a land death has forgotten to visit
and I am not one of his angels.

In a snug room

He sips from his glass, thinking complacently
of the events of the day:
a flattering reference to him in the morning papers,
lunch with his cronies, a profitable deal
signed on the dotted line, a donation sent
to his favourite charity.

And he smiles,
thinking of the taxi coming
with his true love in it.

Everything's fine.

And Nemesis slips two bullets
into her gun
in case she misses with the first one.

That journey

To make a mark
from the mountain horizon to the sea:
a straight line.

It goes through lochs and fields
and fistfuls of villages.
It goes in the dark and the light.

In the harbour a boat
sets its white sail.
Its anchor crawls aboard.

Those who are left behind
will look out to sea,
their eyes bright with hope –

not knowing when it returns
they'll see approaching
a black sail on the bright water.